Pendulum Dowsing

The complete guide to pendulum dowsing, divination, and more!

Table Of Contents

Introduction iii
Chapter 1 – What is Pendulum Dowsing? 1
Chapter 2 – Is Pendulum Dowsing Right For You? 3
Chapter 3 – Essential Items For Pendulum Dowsing 4
Chapter 4 – Ten Suggested Steps to begin Pendulum Dowsing 5
Chapter 5 – Ten things you should remember when divining with a crystal pendulum 11
Chapter 6 – A Basic Overview Of Crystals And Their Effects 16
Chapter 7 – Divination 21
Conclusion 24

Introduction

I want to thank you and congratulate you for downloading the book, *"Pendulum Dowsing"*.

This book contains helpful information about pendulum dowsing, what it is, and how it works!

Pendulum dowsing is a form of dowsing that has been around for thousands of years. Dowsing is a divination skill used primarily for finding water. However, this skill can also be used to find precious minerals, hidden items, answer questions, and even to provide advice!

Pendulum dowsing is primarily used to answer yes/no questions that you may have. This book explains how to create your own pendulum to dowse with, and also how it should be used.

This book will explain to you tips and techniques that will allow you to successfully understand and begin using pendulum dowsing from home! While pendulum dowsing can take some practice to become proficient at, anyone can give it a go.

With the strategies provided within this book, you'll be able to use pendulum dowsing effectively in no time!

Thanks again for downloading this book. **I hope you enjoy it!**

Chapter 1 – What is Pendulum Dowsing?

What is Dowsing?

Dowsing is an old practice used by ancient people to locate items or water in their environment. In terms of other unconventional uses, it has also been used to guide people to make daily decisions or to determine if someone is telling the truth or not.

Now for these methods (especially dowsing for water or for hidden objects), what is usually used is a branch which is almost triangular in its natural state, or a pair of rods held one in each hand. The dowser, or the person performing the dowsing, walks around loosely holding on to the branch or pair of rods in a location where water or the hidden object is suspected to be. This is often a process that involves a lot of trial and error and it is quite tedious, noting that the dowser has to walk around for quite a bit in a specific location.

Now that's dowsing on a larger scale.

There are other ways to dowse though and they can be for more specific reasons. This is where pendulum dowsing comes in.

Pendulum dowsing is a method of dowsing done using a pendulum. Now, most professional pendulum dowsers use a gem or crystal suspended on a light chain or special string, but you can actually do it using anything lying around in your house.

The charts used for pendulum dowsing are also readily available in shops that offer mystical items, or you can just save some money and download one online. There are also some specialty websites that deal with the occult that will sell both the pendulum and the chart to you at very low prices with delivery to your doorstep included.

So with that, it means anyone can start this serious hobby at any time so long as the right resources are available.

Chapter 2 – Is Pendulum Dowsing Right For You?

The next question that you should probably ask is: "is pendulum dowsing right for me?"

Well that really depends on your answer to the next question: Would you trust your daily decisions based on the movement of an inanimate object?

Most people would probably say no.

But if you said yes, then you're most likely to have some luck with the art of pendulum dowsing.

Much like flipping a coin, pendulum dowsing is based on the probability of your dowsing tool to land on either "yes" or "no" or in the case of your penny, heads or tails. In the case of pendulum dowsing, you will need to believe in it in order to get some results.

But why is that so?

Pendulum dowsing relies heavily on our subconscious mind dictating our micro muscles to exert minute vibrations to affect the swinging of the pendulum. In order for it to work, you have to believe fully in the power of the pendulum to come up with answers to your questions.

Although there are many factors attributed towards how the pendulum swings, it is most likely connected to our subconscious and our micro muscle movement. Others claim that electromagnetic waves plays a part in affecting the pendulum, and others would say that spirits can make it move. Whatever the case may be, the pendulum does swing and it does seem to provide answers whenever there is a need to ask for clarity.

Chapter 3 – Essential Items For Pendulum Dowsing

Although dowsing employs different types of divining items, we are going to focus solely on pendulum dowsing. So logically we are going to need a pendulum for this.

Your pendulum is normally going to be suspended on a string or a chain.

A pendulum is normally any gem or crystal, but experts say that you can actually use any thing as a substitute. The reason why most professional practitioners use specific gems or crystals as their pendulum is because of the energy these things possess. Some professional dowsers also claim that certain gems or crystals help them to tune in better and get more specific answers.

Whatever the case may be, as a beginner you can start out with any regular object lying around in your home. For example: a nut suspended on a string is an inexpensive pendulum to start with. As soon as you get better at pendulum dowsing you can progress towards crystals and gems.

The Dowsing Tools

1. A Pendulum (whether it is made of simple materials or crystals and gems doesn't matter to begin with)
2. A Pendulum chart (whether handmade, bought or downloaded from the Internet, doesn't matter either)
3. A clear mind
4. A quiet area to dowse in, preferably with dim candle light to provide a soothing atmosphere (light instrumental music is optional if that gets you in the mood)

And now, you're ready to go!

Chapter 4 – Ten Suggested Steps to begin Pendulum Dowsing

Step 1 – Enter a meditative state.

Relax.

This is the most crucial step in beginning your pendulum dowsing session. You may have all of the items needed to start a session but if you're not relaxed, your session will go to waste.

Experienced dowsers, especially the ones dealing with pendulums, can enter a meditative state within seconds if they need to perform pendulum dowsing. For the uninitiated, here's a way for you to be able to relax within seconds.

First you will need a room that is as quiet as possible with little to no traffic coming in. Next, sit down as comfortably as you can, close your eyes and then start breathing deeply to slowly enter the alpha (or prayerful) state. Take slow deep breaths and as you progress try to make them even slower. At the same time, try to get rid of all the thoughts that bother you.

NOTE: Some practitioners think of a black wall devoid of any details to quickly remove any other thoughts that might impede their descent into a meditative state.

Step 2 – Bring in the pendulum and chart

With your thumb and first finger, hold the string or chain of your pendulum. As a basic rule of thumb, allowing a string length of around three inches should be enough. The length of the string or chain will affect how slow or how fast the pendulum will swing so find a string length that you are comfortable with and stick with it.

Next, hold your pendulum over the center your chart.

Step 3 – Making your pendulum respond to "YES"

In order for the pendulum to start swinging, you will initially have to make it move with a slight movement from your hand and fingers.

For starters, swing the pendulum ever so slightly towards the "YES" portion of your chart and expect it to continue swinging without any further assistance from you.

Ask it out loud to continue swinging as if you were asking another person to perform the act. If it stops, just go on right ahead and restart the process of manually moving it and allowing the crystal to continue on its own afterwards.

NOTE: This may take some time but hopefully you're already in a meditative state so you should have enough patience to get over this hurdle.

Step 4 – Making your pendulum respond to "NO"

Repeat the same process but this time, direct your pendulum towards the "NO" portion of your chart.

The "NO" portion of your chart should be directly opposite to the "YES" portion.

Step 5 – making your pendulum swing to the "Next Question"

Once your pendulum is already responding to your request for it to follow instructions; ask for it to swing in a counter clockwise manner from "No" to "Yes" and then move on to the "Next Question" or "Ready" portion.

Step 6 – Testing your pendulum's level of responsiveness

The next thing to ask your pendulum is for it to head back from one portion of your chart to the other, with precision and right after you ask it to.

NOTE: asking your pendulum to do one thing is different from commanding it to do so. If you've noticed, we used the word "ask". This allows you and your pendulum to work together in harmony instead of you commanding it to do one thing which may affect the results of the dowsing session.

Keep on practicing going from one portion of your chart to the other until you get the hang of it.

Step 7 – Programming your pendulum

Like any computer program that you are going to start using for the first time, programming your crystal or your pendulum to respond accurately is crucial.

If you've followed the instructions provided for the last couple of steps, by now, your confidence and skill level in dowsing should have risen enough for you to be able to start programming your pendulum to work with you.

Now there are three ways to ask your pendulum, and you have to program these questions in.

1. "Pendulum, Can I..."

   The "can I" question effectively asks the pendulum if you are ready to start dowsing in a specific area. It also asks if your level of readiness is enough to have any success dowsing in that area.

   This basically asks your capabilities and your pendulum may or may not give you a positive answer depending on your skill level.

2. "Pendulum, May I..."

   Once your pendulum has determined that you have enough skill to handle pendulum dowsing, you can start with using the "pendulum, may I..." questions.

   This effectively poses the question to your pendulum if you have enough permission to continue or be involved in specific undertakings.

3. "Pendulum, Should I..."

   The "pendulum should I..." question should only be posed if the "pendulum, can I..." or "pendulum, may I" questions are no longer answered.

   This is only to be used as a last resort and should be avoided as much as possible as this type of question pushes the pendulum to answer too hard.

NOTE: These three manners of questioning should help you program your crystal in a way that allows both of you to work together in harmony. Programming should be done in a manner that will make it conducive for you and your crystal to listen to each other.

Step 8 – Checking if your programming worked and basic troubleshooting

As we've mentioned, your crystal needs programming for you to start working with it. Like with a computer, you will need to perform a diagnostic examination to see if it is working and provide the necessary troubleshooting to make your program work.

First, you need to check on your crystal and ask if the programming you performed on it worked. If it says "YES" then you're good to go. Now, if it says "NO", you will have to perform your programming again.

Ask your crystal questions as to why the programming did not work until you determine what the concern area is. You may have to come up with a more specific programming method in order for you to work with your crystal and not use a generic one.

Step 9 – Testing your pendulum dowsing ability

Once you've finished all of the steps above, it's time to start practicing with test questions that you definitely know the answers to. These questions can be anything ranging from "is this my home?" or "am I sitting down now". The key is, these questions are absolutes and you know the answer to them.

This will help you gauge the accuracy of your crystal pendulum and also help you see at what level your dowsing is.

Like any art, pendulum dowsing requires some practice, so try to put in 5 to 10 minutes every day for you to become good at it.

Step 10 – Trusting your pendulum dowsing abilities

As time goes on, you will become better at pendulum dowsing and your confidence level in your crystal should raise enough for you to comfortably dowse at any given time.

Continue practicing all of the above steps mentioned and you should reach a point where it will become easy for you to start a dowsing session with very minimal effort - from entering a meditative state to posing the questions.

Remember not to push your pendulum too hard. Warm up with a few test questions before going into the actual pendulum dowsing session in order for your crystal to warm up enough to handle the task.

Chapter 5 – Ten things you should remember when divining with a crystal pendulum

The world is made up of laws that we should not break. As such, there are also laws associated with pendulum dowsing. Here is the top ten list of things to remember if you're serious about pendulum dowsing.

1. **Be objective at all times**

    When working with your dowsing tools, there will come periods of time when you will need to step back and remove yourself from the situation in order to not affect it on a personal level.

    Be objective in your approach so as not to tamper with your crystal pendulum's energy in its search for the right answer. Patience will play a huge part in this matter.

2. **Protect yourself at all times**

    Dowsing involves a lot of energy detection and manipulation. Sometimes as a conduit of energy we may become affected by the influx of too many waves coming at us from all directions. This means we have opened ourselves way too much to handle the energy coming in.

    This is the reason why you must protect yourself at all times. Use crystals that can help absorb excess energy in order for you to be able to concentrate on the task at hand which is to dowse properly.

3. **Ask absolute questions**

   Although you are encouraged to talk to your crystal pendulum in a manner that seems like you're talking to another person or a friend, understand that there are only limited options from which it can derive its answers from.

   Let's face it, a chart can only provide so many options and your crystal can only swing to a certain number of answers. It can neither expound on the answer it has given nor offer an explanation to the "how's" and "whys" of its answers.

   In order to get a definite answer, pose an absolute question or a close ended question. These are questions that can only be answered with a "Yes" or a "No".

4. **Avoid interfering with the laws of the universe**

   Every one of us has a pre-determined path and the karmic law dictates that whatever we put out there will come back to us ten-fold. In matters like these, never interfere with what the universe has in store for the people you are dowsing for. We can only help to a certain point but to completely change their destiny or fate may prove disastrous in the end!

5. **Respect the privacy of others**

   Pendulum dowsing will allow you to open up a world of information which others may not be privy to. Other people will also come to you eventually to have themselves dowsed. It is in your best interest to practice strict confidentiality at all times in order to retain the trust these people have given to you.

Never, ever, ever dowse another person without their permission as it is akin to invasion of privacy!

6. **Respect the Karmic Law.**

    Most people understand the laws of Karma. But here's an overview: The Karmic law refers to the opposing forces in the universe and if you tip one end of the scale, you are bound to get the effect of the other scale when it is time to balance itself. So it's basically a swing that goes up and down. If you do something today that is positive, something positive will come back in return and if you do something negative, you can expect the same to come back to you.

    So knowing all that, here are some basic tenets that you should hold fast in order to not accept the balance of the universe and always experience good karma.

    1. Always do things with the best interest that are good for others
    2. Avoid using your gifts for purposes of evil or selfish gain
    3. Use your gifts for your needs and the needs of others
    4. Always be grateful for the gifts you possess

    Those 4 should give you extra brownie points in the Karmic law department!

7. **Don't give out medical advice using your pendulum**

    Be careful when somebody asks you for medical advice. Unless you have a medical background and are a licensed physician, diagnosing a medical condition is considered illegal in most states.

    This is not what pendulum dowsing is designed for.

Anyone who comes up to you with an illness or disease should immediately be forwarded to a local health facility and have themselves looked at by medical professionals who are experts in that field.

If they insist, limit your questions to which hospital they should head for, when they should go to the hospital or if they should actually seek the help of a licensed physician. Other than that, steer clear!

8. **Never underestimate the power of sharing**

Art is supposed to be appreciated by the masses. Dowsing in itself is an art and thus needs to be shared as well. Now there is a slight modification to this idea though. Since dowsing is rooted in the occult and sometimes borders on the religious, some people may not be as readily accepting of the idea as others.

To ease the transfer of information, pick a few people you can trust to share this information with at first and slowly work your way up to larger numbers. Remember that we are trying to promote an art form and not turn people off with the idea that it is some form of witchcraft.

9. **Always keep an open mind.**

Dowsing is not a specific science. It relies heavily on probabilities and the outcomes of which are infinite. In order to become good at pendulum dowsing you always have to keep an open eye in order for you to readily absorb new techniques that could help you get more accurate answers or become more proficient in the art.

Gather as much information as you can and look at each piece with as much equality as you can manage in order to weed out the useless data, and focus on what can really help you improve your pendulum dowsing skills.

There are so many avenues of information that you can harvest this data from, so it's highly suggested that you start reading about dowsing and all aspects covered by it, watching videos explaining how dowsing works and the successes of the practitioners, listening to MP3s about dowsing and how to improve your technique, or just plainly going out there to talk to as many people as you can whether they are proficient in dowsing or not.

The amount of information you can gather from these methods should be enough to help you come up with a good idea on how to become the best dowser possible.

10. Keep it Simple

Try to keep all aspects of your dowsing as simple as you can. Be sure to practice and enjoy your dowsing every day.

Chapter 6 – A Basic Overview Of Crystals And Their Effects

All throughout this book, crystals have been mentioned and deemed as essential to pendulum dowsing. Some people swear by it and some believe that they can use other items for their pendulum.

Primarily, crystals are used for ornamentation. They have been used as symbols of power throughout the ages and are valued not only for their beauty, but also for their sacred meanings.

Because of this, people have assigned certain qualities to these crystals. Now, whether crystals do possess some other abilities that affect our moods and energies is still up for speculation.

But if there's one thing that's pretty obvious about crystals, it is perhaps that each unique crystal has a beauty all of its own.

Crystals are extremely popular as jewelry pieces as well. In olden times, crystals were used to adorn the furnishings of kings and priests. These individuals normally had high social standings and were often viewed as very powerful and influential people. Unknowingly, these crystals became associated to these people, and helped convey that sense of power and authority which continues to this day.

Crystals are very powerful because their structures can absorb, conserve, emit or even focus, electromagnetic energy! This is actually being debated as the reason why crystals seem to possess so many qualities that affect not only the mental aspect of humanity but also the physical and spiritual aspect. Whatever it may be, crystals do seem to have an inner strength and power that certain people can easily associate with and use.

Crystals also seem to protect people from harm, and last but not the least; crystals are believed by many to heal people.

This is still under speculation and obviously it's up to you to decide where your personal beliefs lie.

Nonetheless, here are the different colored crystals and what they are believed to do:

Red Crystals

Red denotes physical stimulation and sexual arousal. It also encourages action, boosts our energy, and directly affects our lust and strength.

Examples of red crystals are: carnelian and red jasper

Pink crystals

Pink crystals are softer in appearance and are thus better suited for missions of love, harmony, and sympathy. They're also perfect for self-healing. Some crystals belonging to this group are: Rose quartz, pink tourmaline and rhodochrosite

Orange crystals

Amber and citrine are part of this group of crystal color. These crystals are responsible for stimulating creativity. They're also good for fertility and other organs.

Now if there's one thing that people can immediately relate to when it comes to the color orange; it is a bright and flamboyant color that immediately exudes confidence. So therefore, orange crystals are also used to promote self-confidence.

Yellow crystals

Yellow crystals including the agate, yellow jasper, citrine and amber are also mentally stimulating. This bright color fights depression and helps bridge communication gaps. There is a power that yellow exudes which seems to immediately affect people in a positive manner.

Green crystals

Green crystals exude a certain kind of peacefulness that only they can manage to do. Maybe this is because of the tinge of blue that is present in green. Whatever it is, green crystals are especially sought after because of the way they help to calm people down. This is why green is extensively used in situations where people need to detoxify their minds and bodies.

Crystals like aventurine, moss agate and malachite are excellent examples of this crystal color group.

You can also use green crystals to help you if you have liver problems.

Blue crystals

Blue is perhaps the universal color for calm and relaxation. But aside from that, blue can be used to help a person connect to their inner self easily. Lapis Lazuli which is an excellent crystal to begin with is particularly interesting because it not only promotes tranquility, but it also seems to affect the kidneys and the bladder in a positive manner. Turquoise on the other hand is extensively used by travelers who believe that it provides protection from those who would wish ill on them during long journeys.

If there's one color crystal that you should use for pendulum dowsing, it is this color. Not only does it promote peace and tranquility, but it also allows the diviner to easily connect with their spirits and provide an uplifting journey towards compassion and understanding spiritually and mentally.

In effect, turquoise is the most widely used crystal for amulets and trinkets dating back to ancient times.

Purple crystals

Purple is the color of royalty. Thus it is a good crystal to derive wisdom, clarity, and tolerance from. Amethyst, which is widely known as a purple crystal is especially popular with diviners, since they claim it is a good focal point for spiritual matters. It promotes a high level of brain activity and in effect seems to heighten our natural clairvoyance.

If for no other purpose at all, amethyst is good for meditation. So if you want to get into a meditative state immediately, use an amethyst to focus on. Not only will you reach your alpha state quickly but you'll also be able to help clear your lungs and ease your breathing until you are fully relaxed!

Black crystals

Some people make the immediate association that black is the color for negativity. It may be true in some cases, but for crystals like the onyx or the obsidian, these crystals actually work to absorb negative energy.

Black crystals also help develop a stronger connection to mother Earth.

Brown crystals

Brown crystals are beautiful in their own right for the fact that they possess a warm and natural color. These crystals are generally used in pain elimination. The tiger's eye for example is especially useful during times when arthritic pain is considered unmanageable and extremely painful. Placing one of these crystals on the affected spot seems to have an immediate soothing effect on the sore muscles. So if you're feeling any pain whether it is physical or mental, bring along a brown crystal and allow it to work its magic on your system.

White crystals

White crystals are extensively used for purification purposes. Opal for example is extremely useful in cleansing your body and soul from all the toxins and worries it has acquired over time.

Keeping a section of your home supplied with white crystals will immediately being about a sense of harmony that you can only derive from these naturally occurring minerals. A good combination of white, green and black crystals works even better!

Colorless crystals

Last but not the least: we have the colorless crystals like quartz.

Colorless crystals are especially good for divining purposes as they are extremely useful in clearing our minds and providing a good focus point to direct our energies at.

Chapter 7 – Divination

What is divination?

Basing on the Latin word 'divinare', divination means: "to foresee or to be inspired by a God".

Nowadays, divination has become almost synonymous to occult or ritualistic practices.

As such, divination continues to be considered a pseudo-science and is not readily accepted by the scientific community.

Although that may be the case, divination does seem to have its own rules and regulations, and is often practiced following a rigid ritual.

There are four types of divination according to Julian Jaynes (a noted psychologist who was instrumental in categorizing the divinations).

1. **Omens and omen texts**

    This was started in China and had some practical uses in terms of forecasting and making strategies.
2. **Sortilege (Cleromancy)**

    Sortilege or cleromancy depends heavily on probabilities. The usage of stones, bones, coins and other items was observed in the past. As a direct result, board games and playing cards sprang from this type of divination.

3. **Augury**

    This type of divination relies on shapes and formations as well as the proximity of the divining object to certain elements surrounding it. For example: birds, or more specifically, the flight pattern of birds were used for divination in the past. A more morbid method would be sacrificing animals and taking the liver to determine or forecast the outcome of certain events from the manner in which the blood flowed or spattered. This basically relies heavily on the diviner and how they interpret such phenomena.

4. **Spontaneous**

    This is probably the one most observed by people. This form of divination is basically the generalization of other forms of divination. The diviner basically just reads whatever is readily available to him or her and gives advice based on what they read in their surroundings. Rituals and other objects may or may not be included during this type of divination.

To sum it all up, divination is still basically categorized as a pseudo-science and does not have any solid and reliable proof that it works. There are many instances though of diviners being able to accurately foretell the future or locate hidden items, but there are still many who are skeptical about the veracity of these diviners' claims.

Now the ball is in your corner; whether you believe that divination is a real science or not is entirely up to you. Humans are beings of free will and you have the option to choose right or wrong, good or bad and yes or no. Much like your crystal pendulum, you will head in one direction or the other. You may not be entirely in that direction yet but there are degrees of your persona in that balance.

Life is after all a delicate balance of opposing forces.

Divination, in effect should be seen as a tool or method you can use to arrange your thoughts, and become more attentive to detail in order to benefit the most from your surroundings. Your crystal pendulum should also help you make final decisions, and last but not the least, as a diviner; you will learn how to ask questions. And these are not just any ordinary questions. These will be questions that focus on getting to the truth immediately and remove all the trappings of a dubious conversation.

Divination can be done through so many methods that listing all of them in one book is going to take up more than a couple of chapters. Still there are a few that are notable for having some practical uses like dowsing for water and of course pendulum dowsing which is helping people all across the world become more in tune to their feelings and surroundings.

 So if it seems like your life is jumbled up and filled with clutter at the moment, maybe you need to hold on to a crystal to serve as a focal point for you, or test out pendulum dowsing to find the answers that you seek!

Conclusion

Thank you again for downloading this book!

I hope this book was able to help you learn more about pendulum dowsing!

The next step is to put this information to use, and begin using the power of pendulum dowsing at home!

Finally, if you enjoyed this book, please take the time to share your thoughts and post a review on Amazon. It'd be greatly appreciated!

Thank you and good luck!

www.ingramcontent.com/pod-product-compliance
Lightning Source LLC
LaVergne TN
LVHW021748060526
838200LV00052B/3540